The Future of International Law

by Lassa Oppenheim

INTRODUCTORY NOTE

In a note prepared in 1915 for the English edition, Professor Oppenheim stated the circumstances under which his tractate on The Future of International Law was undertaken and published.

'This little work,' he said, 'originally written in German, was first published in 1911, under the title Die Zukunft des Vekerrechts (Leipzig: W. Engelmann), as a contribution to the Festschrift offered to Professor Karl Binding. Events which have since happened make it necessary to call the reader's attention to the date of original publication.

'The translation into English has been made by Dr. John Pawley Bate. In accordance with the wish of the author some slight modifications of the original text were made before translation. The numbers of the paragraphs and the marginal summaries do not appear in the original.'

As was his wont with all his publications, Professor Oppenheim had sent the undersigned a copy of the German text. The value of 'this little work', as its author called it, was at once apparent, and he yielded to the suggestion that it be put into English, in order that it might be available to English readers in the four quarters of the globe. It was accordingly translated, set up in type, and was on the point of appearing, when on July 28, 1914, the then Austro-Hungarian Monarchy declared war upon Serbia; on August 1 the then German Empire declared war upon Russia, and two days later against France, violated the neutrality of Luxemburg on the same day, and the neutrality of Belgium on the night of the 3rd and 4th of August--thus beginning the series of wars which, taken together, are commonly called the World War.

Professor Oppenheim subsequently came to the conclusion that it would be better to withhold publication until the end of the war. It was done, and the deposit of ratifications of the Treaty of Versailles on January 10, 1920, removed this obstacle.

It should be said, however, that Professor Oppenheim expressed doubts on more than one occasion as to the desirability of its publication, but he allowed himself to be persuaded that an English version might be of service to the great and worthy cause of international law and of international organization.

Modesty was not the least of his virtues.

From time to time Professor Oppenheim has ventured into the same field. In 1918, in the performance of his duty 'to lay down such rules and suggest such measures as may tend to diminish the evils of war and finally to extinguish war between nations', he delivered three lectures on The League of Nations and its Problems, as holder of the Chair of International Law, founded by Dr. Whewell in the University of Cambridge. As in The Future of International Law, so in the lectures, he started from the Hague Conferences and made the work of The Hague the foundation upon which he would base any scheme of international organization. The epigraph which he put upon the title-page, Festina Lente, indicated the spirit in which he approached his task and the advice which he felt called upon to give to the most casual of his readers. In the lectures he took a step in advance--or backward, according to the point of view--advocating that all members of a league of nations should 'agree to unite their economic, military, and naval forces against any one or more States which resort to arms without submitting their disputes to International Courts of Justice or International Councils of Conciliation'.

In the course of 1919, and after the signature of the Treaty of Versailles on June 28 of that year, Professor Oppenheim contributed to the Revue de droit international public an article in French on The Essential Character of the League of Nations. And what may be considered as his final views on the subject are contained in the third edition of his Treatise on International Law (vol. i, pp. 264-310), the first volume of which appeared in 1920. Professor Oppenheim accepted the League of Nations, but his eyes were open to its defects as well as to its merits.

The partisans of the present League of Nations will prefer Professor Oppenheim's later views, as expressed in his lectures and in the Treatise on International Law. The opponents of the present League of Nations will prefer his earlier views, contained in the present publication. The future will decide which are the more acceptable.

At the Oxford session of the Institute of International Law, held a year to the month before the outbreak of the World War, it was the custom of its members to pass the evenings together in informal discussion of their chosen subject. On one occasion the discussion assumed the form of a dialogue between

Professor Oppenheim on the one hand and Mr. Elihu Root on the other. At an unusually late hour the company broke up, and Mr. Root, putting out his hand to Professor Oppenheim, said, 'Bon soir, cher Ma 頰 re'.

James Brown Scott, Director of the Division of International Law.

WASHINGTON, D.C. February 28, 1921.

CONTENTS

INTRODUCTION

PAGE 1. International law in the past 1 2. No international law in antiquity 1 3. How the conception of a family of nations arose 2 4. The law of nature as the basis of the law of nations 2 5. Positive international law 4 6. International legislation initiated by the Congress of Vienna 4 7. International Administrative Union 5 8. Legislation of the Peace Conferences and of the Naval Conference of London 5 9. The Permanent Court of Arbitration and other international courts 6 10. The Hague Peace Conferences as a permanent institution 6 11. Uncertainty as to the fate of the Declaration of London and of some of the Hague Conventions 7 12. The task of the future 7

CHAPTER I

THE ORGANIZATION OF THE SOCIETY OF STATES

13. Is the law of nations an anarchic law? 9 14. All law is order 9 15. The family of nations is a society ruled by law although it does not as yet possess special organs 10 16. Not necessary that the family of nations should remain an unorganized society 11 17. The pacificist ideal of an organization of the family of nations 11 18. The world-state is not desirable 12 19. The world-state would not exclude war 13 20. War may gradually disappear without a world-state 14 21. Importance of pacificism 15 22. Impossible for the family of nations to organize itself on the model of the state 16 23. Impossible to draft a plan for the complete organization of the family of nations 16 24. The Permanent Court of Arbitration the nucleus of the future organization of the family of nations 17 25. The Hague Peace Conferences as organs of the family of nations 17 26. Outlines of a constitution of the family of nations 18 27. The proposed constitution leaves state-sovereignty intact 20 28. The equality of states 20 29. Absence of any executive power 21

CHAPTER II

INTERNATIONAL LEGISLATION

30. Quasi-legislation within the domain of international law 23 31. Hague

Peace Conferences as an organ for international legislation 24 32. Difficulties in the way of international legislation. The language question 25 33. The opposing interests of the several states 25 34. Contrasted methods of drafting 25 35. These difficulties distinct from those due to carelessness. Article 23 (h) of the Hague Regulations of land war is an example 27 36. The German and the English interpretation of Article 23 (h) 27 37. Davis's interpretation of Article 23 (h) 28 38. Impossible to reconcile the divergent views about Article 23 (h) 29 39. Difficulties due to the fact that international law cannot be made by a majority vote, or repealed save by a unanimous vote. A way out found in the difference between universal and general international law 30 40. International laws which are limited in point of time 31 41. International legislation no longer to be left to mere chance 33 42. The Declaration of London thoroughly prepared beforehand 34 43. The preparation of the Declaration a pattern for future international legislation 34 44. Intentionally incomplete and fragmentary laws 35 45. Interpretation of international statutes 35 46. International differences as regards interpretation 36 47. Different nations have different canons of interpretation 37 48. Controverted interpretation of the Declaration of London an example 37 49. Some proposals for the avoidance of difficulties in interpretation 39

CHAPTER III

INTERNATIONAL ADMINISTRATION OF JUSTICE

50. Law can exist without official administration 41 51. The Hague Court of Arbitration as a permanent institution 41 52. The proposed International Prize Court and Court of Arbitral Justice 42 53. Does the constitution of the International Prize Court violate the principle of the equality of states? 43 54. Does the International Prize Court restrict the sovereignty of the several states? 43 55. Would the formation of an international Prize Court of Appeal infringe the sovereignty of the several states? 44 56. The powers of the International Prize Court do not curtail state-sovereignty 45 57. Difference between international courts of arbitration and real international courts of justice 46 58. Fundamentals of arbitration in contradistinction to administration of justice by a court 47 59. Opposition to a real international court 48 60. A real international court does not endanger the peaceable settlement of disputes 49 61. Composition of an international court 50 62. International courts of appeal a necessity 51 63. Are international courts valueless if states are not bound to

submit their disputes to them? 52 64. What is to be done if a state refuses to accept the decision of an international court? 54 65. Executive power not necessary for an international court 54 66. Right of intervention by third states and war as ultima ratio 55

CHAPTER IV

THE SCIENCE OF INTERNATIONAL LAW

67. New tasks for the science of international law 56 68. The science of international law must become positive 56 69. The science of international law must be impartial 58 70. The science of international law must free itself from the tyranny of phrases 58 71. The meaning of 'Kriegsr鋂 on geht vor Kriegsmanier' 59 72. The doctrine of Rousseau concerning war 60 73. The science of international law must become international 63 74. Necessary to consult foreign literature on international law 63 75. Necessary to understand foreign juristic methods 64

CONCLUSION

76. The aims defended are not Utopian 66 77. Obstacles to progress 67

INTRODUCTION

[Sidenote: International law in the past.]

1. He who would portray the future of international law must first of all be exact in his attitude towards its past and present. International law as the law of the international community of states, such as is the present-day conception of it, is of comparatively modern origin. Science dutifully traces it back to Hugo Grotius as its father. In his immortal work on the Law of War and of Peace he, with masterly touch, focalizes (as it were) all the tendencies which asserted themselves during the latter half of the middle ages into a law between independent states, in such sort that all subsequent development goes back to him. Undoubtedly the roots of this law reach back into the remotest past of civilization, for independent states, nay, independent tribes too, cannot

have more or less frequent dealings with each other without developing definite forms therefor. And so the immunity which must everywhere be conceded to ambassadors and heralds will probably be the oldest root of international law.

[Sidenote: No international law in antiquity.]

2. But all attempts to find in the ancient world a law of the same kind as modern international law must inevitably come to grief on the fact that the idea of a community of law between civilized states was entirely foreign to antiquity, and only begins to make its gradual appearance in the last third of the middle ages. The Jewish ideal of perpetual peace and the union of all mankind under One God, foreseen in prophetic vision by Isaiah (ii. 2-4), may be taken as the first formulation of pacificist doctrine, which of course implies a community of law between all states, but the prophet does not apprehend this community of law as an independent idea. This idea was likewise unknown in its generality to Greek civilization, although certainly looming before it with some clearness in the international relations of the Greek city-states one to another. But even if we may speak of a law resembling in many respects modern international law as prevailing between the states of ancient Greece, this law must nevertheless be limited to Greek states, foreign states and peoples standing outside this community of law as barbarians. On the other hand, Roman law possessed, it is true, a mass of legal rules for the intercourse between the Roman Empire and all foreign states, but these rules were Roman law and not rules of an international law such as postulates an international community of law.

[Sidenote: How the conception of a family of nations arose.]

3. The idea of an international community of law could not have obtained acceptance before a time when there existed a number of completely independent states, internally akin in virtue of a community of intensive civilization and continually brought into contact with one another by a lively intercourse. It was in this way that an international community of law was begotten at the end of the middle ages out of Christian civilization and mutual intercourse. Grotius and his forerunners would not have been able to create international law, had not the conception of a community of law between Christian states enjoyed a general recognition, and had not international

intercourse before their day evolved already a large number of rules of intercourse, which were based on custom and in part on very ancient usages.

[Sidenote: The law of nature as the basis of the law of nations.]

4. A theoretical basis for the erection of a system of international law was provided by the law of nature. This likewise is duteously traced back by science to Grotius, although in this department also he stands on the shoulders of his predecessors. The riddle, how it was possible to find a foundation for international law (as also for constitutional law and other branches of law) in the law of nature, which itself reposed upon so unstable a basis, is easy of solution for those who contemplate the historical development of all law with minds clear from prejudice. The contention of the historical school that all law springs up 'naturally', like language, is chimerical. Wherever a demand for law and order imperiously asserts itself, rules of law arise there. Every epoch of history produces alike that mode of legal development which it needs and that theoretical basis therefor which corresponds to its own interpretation of the nature of things. Accordingly the growth of law is everywhere dependent on, or at least influenced by, a conscious or unconscious creation of law. Custom, usage, habit, religion, morality, the nature of the thing, tradition, reason, the examples of single individuals, and many other factors, contribute the material out of which the requisite rules of law are built up. Where a strong central authority busies itself, year in year out, with legislation, expressly enacted law naturally takes the foremost place, and customary law makes itself felt to a less and less degree. But where such a strong central authority does not exist or does not busy itself with continuous legislation, then the above-named factors exercise a more direct influence upon the development of law, should there arise in actual life an imperious demand for definite rules of law. The theory of natural law was only the mirror held up by legal philosophy, in which the rays emitted by these factors were focused into a homogeneous image.

[Sidenote: Positive international law.]

5. That, by the side of his international law, with its basis in natural law, there was also a positive international law, was not unrecognized by Grotius, but his purpose was merely to depict a system of international law which should compel universal observance irrespective of time and nation. And shortly after Grotius, Zouche and his followers did indeed attempt, in opposition to him, to

formulate just such a positive international law, but it could not win for itself, at any rate in the seventeenth century, any great recognition; development was overshadowed by the system of Grotius, and many of his rules of natural law gradually obtained recognition in practice as customary law. But the increasing intercourse of states in the eighteenth century called forth a more positive school of international jurists, and the works of Bynkershoek, Moser, and Martens fertilized the soil on which in the nineteenth century there could gradually grow a really positive theory of international law, even if the scales which betoken its past connexion with natural law still adhere to the international law of to-day.

[Sidenote: International legislation initiated by the Congress of Vienna.]

6. A positive theory of international law was demanded by the fact that in the first quarter of the nineteenth century, with the Final Act of the Congress of Vienna, the quasi-legislative activity of international conventions asserted itself for the first time. From then onwards, general international law was frequently evolved by means of an international convention. It was in this way that the permanent neutralization of Switzerland, Belgium, and Luxemburg was effected, the navigation of the so-called international rivers in Europe declared free, the slave-trade abolished, the grades of diplomatic agents regulated, privateering abolished, the necessity of effectiveness in a blockade recognized, the principle 'free ships, free goods' finally established, neutral goods on enemy ships declared free, rules provided in the interest of those wounded in battle, explosive bullets under the weight of 400 grammes forbidden, the Suez Canal neutralized, and so forth.

[Sidenote: International Administrative Union.]

7. Another fact of great importance is the endeavour, which first manifested itself in the World Postal Union of 1874, to carry out the international administration of common interests, economic and other, by means of more or less general international unions. In this way a series of international administrative unions, often conjoined with special international boards, have been called into existence.

[Sidenote: Legislation of the Peace Conferences and of the Naval Conference of London.]

8. With the end of the nineteenth and the first decade of the twentieth century, in which occur the first and second Peace Conferences at The Hague and the Naval Conference of London, the development of international law enters upon a new and pregnant epoch. If hitherto, despite the momentous law-making treaties of the nineteenth century, international law was essentially a book-law, a system erected by greater or smaller authorities on the foundations of state practice and in its details often uncertain and contested, it is now subjected more and more, and in a wide domain, to the legislating influence of law-making international conventions. To mention only the principal matters: A code has been issued which, full of lacunae as it is, nevertheless encompasses the whole area of land war; it has been laid down that war shall only be begun by a declaration of war; the employment of force for the recovery of contract-debts has been forbidden; the rights and duties of neutrals in land war and naval war, the treatment of enemy merchant vessels at the outbreak of hostilities, and the conditions of the conversion of merchant vessels into men-of-war have been legislatively fixed; rules concerning the laying of submarine mines, concerning bombardment by naval forces in time of war, concerning the application of the principles of the Geneva Convention to naval warfare, concerning certain limitations on the right of prize in naval warfare have been agreed on; many states have concurred in a prohibition of the discharge of explosive missiles from air-ships; and a code of the rules of naval warfare, so far as it touches the trade of neutrals, dealing with the topics of blockade, contraband of war, unneutral service, destruction of neutral prizes, sale of enemy merchantmen to neutrals, enemy property, convoy and so forth, has been agreed on, though still unratified.

[Sidenote: The Permanent Court of Arbitration and other international courts.]

9. It is noteworthy that the first Hague Conference established a permanent international arbitral tribunal and that the second Hague Conference decided on the establishment of an International Prize Court and produced a plan for a standing international court at The Hague. Hitherto there have been no international courts for the decision of disputes, and if contending powers have been ready to refer their disputes to arbitration, they have always first had to form an arbitral tribunal; but now there is in existence an actual International Court of Arbitration, and other international courts are in contemplation.

10. Lastly, it is noteworthy that in the Final Act of the second Hague Conference a recommendation was expressed that the powers should call a third Conference in the year 1915, and two years before its meeting should appoint a preparatory committee, entrusted, among other things, with the task of proposing a system of organization and procedure for the coming Conference. This recommendation gives the first impetus towards making the Hague Conferences a permanent institution and so ensuring their periodic assembly without the need of initiative on the part of some one power or another.

11. Neither all the results of the second Hague Peace Conference nor those of the London Naval Conference are as yet assured, for the Declaration of London has not yet been ratified, and so the fate of the International Prize Court is still involved in doubt. The fate of some of the numerous conventions of the second Hague Conference is still in similar doubt, and many of those conventions which have been ratified present only a fragmentary and provisional settlement of their respective topics. Whatever may be the fate of these agreements which are still in suspense, this much is certain, that international legislation, international administration of justice, and international organization occupy the foreground of affairs, have already been in part established, and must be in ever-increasing requisition by the present and the coming generation.

12. If in the following pages I undertake the discussion of these three weighty matters, it is entirely foreign to my purpose to peer into the future with the eyes of prophecy or to busy my fancy with building castles in the air. What I propose is only to place in clear light the problems which are now coming into view and to furnish some indications which may contribute to their successful solution. If it is only to happy accident that we owe the assembling of the Peace Conferences, and likewise the issues of the same, we must all the more attempt in the future to assure success by dint of careful deliberation,

systematic preparation, and a purposeful consideration of the problems which press for attention. And the science of international law must bethink itself and devote itself, with a more exact method than has hitherto been usual, to the elaboration of the results of past and future Conferences and to the incorporation of them in its system.

CHAPTER I

THE ORGANIZATION OF THE SOCIETY OF STATES

[Sidenote: Is the law of nations an anarchic law?]

13. International legislation and administration presuppose the existence of law and order within the society of states, and this latter topic must therefore be treated before the former. International law has been called 'anarchic law' on the ground that hitherto the society of states has not been organized and that it must ever remain unorganized on account of the complete sovereignty of its members. It seems to me that this position is untenable. The idea of anarchy forms a contrast to that of law. Law can as little be anarchic as anarchy can be an institute of law. The conception of the one excludes the other. He who cannot conceive of law apart from a superior power enforcing it on its subjects, may perhaps call the international society of states anarchic, but then he will also have to contest the existence of an international law, and, logically, he should also deny the possibility of the existence of an international society.

[Sidenote: All law is order.]

14. He, however, who identifies law and order, and who, whenever he finds in any society rules making their appearance which are conceived as compulsory for the conduct of its members, speaks of law--in contrast to morality, the observance of which is left to the conscience of the members-- will also be able to speak of law in a society where there is no relation of superior and subject, provided only that the relation between the members is regulated in an ordered manner. That the international society of states is orderly regulated after this wise will be denied by no one who looks at it without prejudice, and who does not confuse order in a society with order of such a kind as is maintained by special organs of the society in question.

[Sidenote: The family of nations is a society ruled by law although it does not as yet possess special organs.]

15. The admission that hitherto the international society of states has not possessed any special organs, is not an admission that it has not been an ordered society. Quite the contrary is the case, for numerous rules may be pointed to which show that that society is an ordered one. There are the rules which relate to the independence of each state of all other states, to the equality of all states, to their supremacy both personal and territorial, and to their responsibility; and in addition there are those rules which, exceptionally, allow, or at any rate excuse, certain inroads on the legal sphere of other states. And the admission that hitherto this society has possessed no permanent special organs is not an admission that no ways and means are available for the maintenance of existing order and for the formation of more thoroughgoing order, and for the development of a quasi-legislative and administrative activity. Here, too, quite the contrary is the case. Every state has possessed and possesses numerous organs for its international relations, these relations are governed by international conventions and international custom, and numerous congresses and conferences assemble from time to time, when it is a question of making international arrangements of a more general character. In this way it has been possible, even without permanent organs of the international society, to increase and multiply the rules of the law of this society. It does not follow, however, that this society would not attain its aims better than in the past, if it were able to convert itself from an unorganized into an organized society.

[Sidenote: Not necessary that the family of nations should remain an unorganized society.]

16. The assertion that, because of the unlimited sovereignty of its members, the family of nations must remain for all time an unorganized society, either has in view the organization of international society on the model of a state, or is founded on an untenable conception of the idea of sovereignty. If the compression of the whole world into the form of a single state were attained, the states of the day would certainly lose their sovereignty and be degraded into provinces. On the other hand, however, the sovereignty of the members of the international society just as little excludes its organization as the fact of the existence of this society excludes the sovereignty of its members. Sovereignty

as the highest earthly authority, which owes allegiance to no other power, does not exclude the possibility that the sovereign should subject himself to a self-imposed order, so long as this order does not place him under any higher earthly power. All members of the international society thus subject themselves in point of fact to the law of nations without suffering the least diminution of their sovereignty. But of course, for him to whom sovereignty is equivalent to unrestrained power and unlimited arbitrariness of conduct, there cannot be any international law at all, any more than any constitutional law, seeing that international and constitutional law are opposed to absolute arbitrariness, even though they recognize that a sovereign state is the highest earthly authority.

[Sidenote: The pacificist ideal of an organization of the family of nations.]

17. Hitherto, the demand for an organization of the international society has always issued from the pacificist party, in order to render the suppression of war possible. In the struggle round the pacificist ideal the chief objection has always been the absence of any judicial authority over states, and of any supreme executive power, able to compel, in a dispute between states, the execution of a judicial decree. Accordingly it has been the aim of the pacificists to obtain an organization of the international society, such as would compress the whole world, or at least whole parts of the world, such as Europe and America, into the form of a federal state or a system of confederated states. The belief is that only in this way can war be got rid of as a mode of settling disputes between states, and thereby the ever-increasing demands of naval and military budgets be avoided.

[Sidenote: The world-state is not desirable.]

18. Whatever else can be urged against a universal federal state and the like, it is at the present day no longer a physical impossibility. Distance has been so conquered by the telegraph, the railway, and the steamboat, that in fact the annual assembly of a world-parliament would be no impossibility, and in any case a world-government, wherever its seat might be, would be able to secure almost immediate obedience to its behests in the uttermost parts of the earth. There is, indeed, only a quantitative and not a qualitative difference between a command issued by the British government in London to the remotest part of India or Africa, and such a command as, in a federal state comprising the

whole world, would issue to the remotest part of the earth from the central government. Moreover, the ever-increasing international intercourse and its results--the expression 'internationalism', to denote this, is found to-day in all languages--has brought the populations of the various states so near to one another, and has so closely interwoven their interests, that on this ground also the theoretical possibility of erecting and maintaining a world-state of the federal type cannot be denied. But its theoretical and physical possibility prove absolutely nothing as regards its utility and desirability. In spite of all my sympathy with the efforts of my idealistic pacificist friends, it is my firm conviction that the world-state is in no form practically useful or desirable, for it would bring death instead of life. So far as we can foresee, the development of mankind is inseparably bound up with the national development of the different peoples and states. In these conditions variety brings life, but unity brings death. Just as the freedom and competition of individuals is needed for the healthy progress of mankind, so also is the independence and rivalry of the various nations. A people that is split up into different states may attain its national development better in a federal state than in a unitary state, and smaller nations and fragments of nations may (let us admit) develop better when combined into one state which has grown up historically out of several nationalities, than each would do in a state of its own, but the rule nevertheless remains, that strong nations can develop successfully only in an entirely independent and self-supported state of their own.

[Sidenote: The world-state would not exclude war.]

19. Further, it is by no means sure that war would necessarily disappear from a world-state. The example of the duel is instructive here. Although forbidden in all civilized states and threatened with penalties, it--certain states excepted-- continues to flourish. Enactments being impotent where the public sentiment of the dominant class refuses them any moral recognition, the duel will not disappear so long as the moral attitude of the circles concerned demands it as a protection for personal honour. And the Sonderbund war of 1847 in Switzerland, the American war of secession from 1861 to 1865, and the Austro-Prussian war of 1866 within the German Bund, show that organization into a confederation of states or into a federal state does not necessarily banish war.

[Sidenote: War may gradually disappear without a world-state.]

20. On the other hand, the gradual disappearance of war, which certainly is a correct ideal, is to be hoped for and expected quite apart from any development of a world-state, even if neither to-day nor to-morrow can be contemplated for the complete realization of this ideal. Many states have already entered into numerous agreements with other individual states to refer to arbitration disputed questions of law and questions about the interpretation of treaties, so far as these disputed questions do not touch the vital interests, independence, or honour of the parties. It is here that further development must begin. The man who is not a victim to prejudice asks the reasonable question, why should vital interests and the independence and honour of states necessarily be withdrawn from the domain of judicial decision? If individuals in a state submit themselves to the judge's sentence, even when their vital interests, their honour, their economic independence, aye, and their physical existence are in issue, why should it be impossible for states to do the same? If only we succeeded in the clear enunciation of legal rules for all international relations; if only we could succeed in finding independent and unbiased men to whose judgment a state could confidently submit its cause; if only we could succeed in bringing such men together in an independent international court-- there would then be no reason why the great majority of states should not follow the example of the very small minority which has already agreed to settle all possible disputes by means of arbitration. The objection that a state could not submit its honour, for example, to the sentence of a judge is as little entitled to recognition as is the claim, made by those dominant classes which in many states glorify the duel, that men of honour could not settle an affair of their honour by means of a judge's decree. As long as public sentiment concerning international relations remains rooted in its present position, it must be confessed that there can be no talk of any progress, just as the duel also will not disappear as long as there is no success in bringing about a change of moral attitude on the part of the classes concerned. But by degrees obsolete moral positions are undermined by all kinds of influences, then they are abandoned and higher positions are adopted in their stead.

[Sidenote: Importance of pacificism.]

21. It is here that the importance and value of the modern pacificist movement emerge with clearness. Wide circles are caught by this movement, even the governments of all countries are no longer able to hold aloof from its

influence, and its opponents too can no longer fight it with nothing but scorn and ridicule. Whoever is a believer in the unlimited progress of civilization will also believe that a time must come when all states will freely bind themselves to submit all disputes to judicial or arbitral decision. General disarmament will not hasten the dawn of this day, for it can only arrive through the deepening of the public sentiment with reference to international relations. General disarmament will not make wars to cease, but the ceasing of war will bring about general disarmament! As already said, not to-day nor to-morrow will this time come; we stand now only at the very beginning of the developments that make for the realization of this ideal. It cannot come to pass unless and until international society develops an organization of a kind ever tending to perfect itself.

[Sidenote: Impossible for the family of nations to organize itself on the model of the state.]

22. How then must and will this organization take shape? The proposals which hitherto have been made for the organization of the world are freaks of fancy. Of notable value as indications of idealistic speculation in the midst of an adverse world, they crumble into dust immediately they are soberly scrutinized. All proposals which aim at the organization of international society after the pattern of the organization of the state--whether a unitary state or a federal state, or a system of confederated states--are either impracticable or do not meet the needs of the case. Every organization of the community of states must take as its starting-point the full sovereignty and the absolute equality of states, and must preserve these characters intact. There can, therefore, be no talk of a political central authority standing above individual states; and so the organization in question must be sui generis and cannot frame itself on the model of state organization.

[Sidenote: Impossible to draft a plan for the complete organization of the family of nations.]

23. It is, however, impossible to draft at the present time the plan of such a complete organization in its details or even in mere outline. The growth and final shaping of the international organization will go hand in hand with the progress of the law of nations. Now the progress of the law of nations is conditioned by the growth of the international community in mental strength,

and this growth in mental strength in its turn is conditioned by the growth in strength and in bulk, the broadening and the deepening, of private and public international interests, and of private and public morale. In the nature of the case this progress can mature only very slowly. We have here to do with a process of development lasting over many generations and probably throughout centuries, the end of which no man can foresee. It is enough for us to have the beginning of the development before our eyes and, so far as our strength and insight extend, to have the opportunity of trying to give it its appropriate aim and direction. More we cannot do. Much, if not all, depends on whether the international interests of individual states become stronger than their national interests, for no state puts its hand to the task of international organization save when, and so far as, its international interests urge it more or less irresistibly so to do.

[Sidenote: The Permanent Court of Arbitration the nucleus of the future organization of the family of nations.]

24. I said, we have the beginning of the development before our eyes. It consists in the erection of the Permanent Court of Arbitration at The Hague, and in the permanent Bureau attached thereto. Here we have an institution belonging not to the individual contracting states but to the international society of states in contrast to the individual members, and it is open to the use of all the individual members. If the Declaration of London be ratified, and if (which scarcely admits of doubt) it be adopted by all the states which were not represented at the Conference of London, then the International Prize Court, which was decided on at the second Hague Conference, will become a fact. This Court will also become an organ of the international community. Mention must also be made of the so-called international bureaux of the so-called international unions, which have come into existence in the period beginning with 1874; for some at least of them will develop into organs of international society, although they so far are only organs of the respective special international unions.

[Sidenote: The Hague Peace Conferences as organs of the family of nations.]

25. Reference must in conclusion be made to the Hague Peace Conferences themselves, for it is to be expected that such Conferences will assemble periodically in the future. If success attends the effort to bring all members of

the international community to an agreement, in virtue of which a Hague Peace Conference assembles at periodic intervals without being called together by this or that power, then an organ of international society will have arisen, the value of which none can decry. It will then be possible to say that the international community has become an actually organized society, and it will then be no longer open to doubt that the organization of this society will gradually become more and more developed. Before everything else this at least will then be attained, that an organ of the international society of states, comparable to the parliaments of individual states, will have come into existence, which can attend to international legislation as the needs of the time require, and can cause a continuous growth in the range of matters submitted to international tribunals. All the same, I yield myself to no hot-blooded hope of a speedy realization of Utopian schemes. Even when this organization is already there, progress will be but slight and gradual, and will encounter unceasing opposition. Progress in this department has always to reckon on a conflict with adverse interests and efforts, and it must be expected that in the continuous struggle between international and national interests the latter will only slowly prepare themselves to yield.

[Sidenote: Outlines of a constitution of the family of nations.]

26. It is not, however, enough that agreement should make periodic Peace Conferences a permanent institution. The international community must provide itself with a constitution, the ground-plan of which would be something like the following:

1. The society of states is composed of all sovereign states which mutually recognize each other's internal and external independence.

2. Every recognized sovereign state has the right to take part in the Peace Conferences.

3. No state taking part in the Conferences is bound by the resolutions of the Conferences without its assent. Majority resolutions only bind the members of that majority. On the other hand, no state is entitled to require that only such resolutions be adopted as it assents to.

4. Every participant state has the right to be heard at the Conferences, to

bring forward proposals, to make motions, and to speak on the proposals and motions of other participants.

5. A standing international commission shall be appointed whose duty it shall be to summon all the members of the international community to the Conferences, to make previous inquiries as to the proposals and motions which are to be brought before the Conference and to inform all participants of them, and to prepare and carry out all other business which the Conferences may from time to time entrust to it.

6. Rules of procedure for the Conferences shall be elaborated, which shall govern the conduct of the proceedings of the Conferences, so that the proceedings can follow a defined course without degenerating into a time-wasting discussion.

7. The question of the presidency of the Conferences shall be settled once for all, so that no room be left for quarrels and jealousies about precedence. It might perhaps be found expedient before every Conference to decide on the presidency by lot.

8. All resolutions come into force only when and so far as they are ratified by the respective states. On the other hand, every state binds itself, once and for all, to carry out in good faith the resolutions which it has ratified.

9. All states bind themselves to submit to the decisions of the international tribunals to which they have appealed, so far as these decisions are within the competence of the respective tribunals.

Something like this would be the ground-plan of a constitution of the international community. Rules 5-7 are demanded by the nature of the case; rules 1-4 and 8-9 contain nothing new, but merely express what observation would show to be the legal position at present.

[Sidenote: The proposed constitution leaves state-sovereignty intact.]

27. It must be particularly remarked that such a constitution can in no way infringe on the full sovereignty of individual states. Apart from the fact that the idea of sovereignty indicates an absolute independence of any higher

earthly power, that idea has never acquired a rigid and uniformly recognized content. Times and circumstances have influenced and shaped it in different states and in the mouths of different authorities. This development of the idea, an idea which has won a place for itself and the retention of which seems desirable despite all opposition, may go further still in the future.

[Sidenote: The equality of states.]

28. The proposed constitution, further, makes no inroad at all on the equality of states. This equality is the indispensable foundation of international society. The idea of equality merely expresses the fact that in all resolutions of the international society every state, whatever may be its size and political importance, obtains one voice and no more than one, that every state can be bound by a resolution only with its consent, and that no state can exercise jurisdiction over another state. It does not and cannot express more. In no circumstances is it to be asserted that unanimity is a condition for all resolutions of the Conferences, and that all resolutions are void to which one or more states refuse their consent. Of course, such resolutions bind those only who assent to them, and of course unanimous resolutions alone can be considered to be universally binding. But nothing should hinder the Conferences--and so it happened in the two first Conferences--from passing majority resolutions. It must never be lost sight of that such majority resolutions do not go to form a universal but only a general law of nations. Only he who repudiates the necessary distinction between a particular and a general and a universal law of nations can demand unanimity. Now the development which up to the present has taken place in the law of nations has shown the necessity of this distinction. It would be extremely difficult to enumerate any large number of universally accepted rules of the law of nations--apart from those which have obtained recognition as customary law. We have only to think of the Declaration of Paris, to which some states still refuse assent. History also teaches us that the general law of nations has a tendency gradually to become the universal law of nations. It is therefore permissible, when a forward step which fails to gain unanimous approval has become a practical matter, for that majority of states which is ready for it to take the step by themselves; the dissenting states will give in their adhesion in course of time. And if and when this should turn out not to be the case, such a majority resolution would anyhow represent, in a narrower circle of international society, a step forward from which there is no obligation to

forbear merely because others are unwilling to join in taking it.

[Sidenote: Absence of any executive power.]

29. This constitution, finally, makes no provision for any kind of executive power, and so it avoids the proposal to set up in international society an organization resembling that of a state. All proposals for an international executive authority run counter not only to the idea of sovereignty, but also to the ideal of international peace and of international law. The aim of this development is not the coercion of recalcitrant states, but a condition of things in which there are no recalcitrant states because every state has freely submitted to the obligation to refer disputes to the international tribunals and to abide by their decision. It is just in this respect that the international community of states differs for all time from the community of individuals who are united into a state, the latter requiring as ultima ratio executive compulsion on the part of a central power, while the former consistently with its nature and definition can never possess such a central power. It will, we must confess, call for a long development before such a condition of things is realized, and, until this realization is effected, war will not disappear but will remain an historic necessity.

CHAPTER II

INTERNATIONAL LEGISLATION

[Sidenote: Quasi-legislation within the domain of international law.]

30. When we speak of legislation we have in view as a rule a state, wherein there is a law-making power which acts without reference to the consent of individual subjects. For even if in a constitutional state an individual does anyhow exercise so much influence upon legislation as comes from voting at the election of members of parliament, still he has no direct influence, and must submit to a law that has been enacted whether he approves of it or not. That is why it is asserted that there cannot be any talk of legislation in the domain of international law. And, in fact, that is so if we adhere rigorously to the meaning of the concept 'legislation', as developed in the domain of internal state life. The nature of the case does not, however, demand so rigid an adherence as this; legislation is really nothing more than the conscious

creation of law in contrast to the growth of law out of custom. And it is an admitted fact that, side by side with international law developed in this latter way, there is an international law which the members of the community of states have expressly created by agreement. We might therefore quite well substitute the term agreeing a law for the term decreeing a law,--but why introduce a new technical term? This international 'agreeing a law' does consciously and intentionally create law, and it is therefore a source of law. And provided that we always bear in mind that this source of law operates only through a quasi-legislative activity, there is no obstacle to speaking, in a borrowed sense, of international 'legislation'. Nevertheless, agreeable and apt as this term is, it must not lead us to assimilate the internal legislation of a state and international legislation save in the one respect that in both law is made in a direct, conscious and purposive manner, in contrast to law that originates in custom.

[Sidenote: Hague Peace Conferences as an organ for international legislation.]

31. International law of the legislative kind existed before the law of the Hague Peace Conferences; it issued from the conventions drawn up from time to time at congresses and conferences. It was a great step forward that the Congress of Vienna was able, for the first time, to create general international law by agreement, and that thereby general international law of the legislative kind could come into existence side by side with the customary law of nations. But the nineteenth century introduced international legislation only occasionally. If, as sketched above, success attends the attempt to make the Hague Peace Conferences a permanent institution, there would be evolved for the society of states a legislative organ corresponding to the parliaments of individual states. A wide field opens thus for further international legislative activity. Even if the time be not ripe for a comprehensive codification of the whole law of nations, there is nevertheless a series of matters in need of international regulation; for example, extradition, the so-called international private law and international criminal law, acquisition and loss of nationality, and a series of other matters, not to mention matters of international administration. Matters which are already governed by customary law might also be brought within the domain of enacted law, and at the same time could be put as regards details upon a surer basis. I have in mind the law of ambassadors and consuls, the law concerning the open sea and territorial waters, the law about merchantmen and men-of-war in foreign territorial

waters, and more of this kind.

[Sidenote: Difficulties in the way of international legislation.]

32. The peculiar character of international legislation involves, however, difficulties of all sorts.

[Sidenote: The language question.]

There is, to begin with, the question of language. Seeing that it is impossible to employ all languages in the enactment of rules of international law, an agreement must be made for adopting some one language for these laws, in the same way that French is used at the present time. But the difficulty thence arising is not insuperable, and is hardly greater than that which is encountered in drafting a treaty between peoples whose speech belongs to different families. It must, however, be a rigid rule that in every case of doubt the text of the law in its original language--not that of a translation into the languages of other countries--is authoritative.

[Sidenote: The opposing interests of the several states.]

33. There is, secondly, the difficulty of contenting the opposite interests of the members of the community of states. But this, too, is in practice not insurmountable. Of course, where there is such a brawling between these interests that no agreement is possible, there can from the outset be no talk of international legislation. This, however, is not everywhere the case. On the contrary, it is often and in different areas the case, that the international interests of states make themselves felt so urgently and so cogently that these states are ready to sacrifice their particular interests if only a reasonable compromise be open to them.

[Sidenote: Contrasted methods of drafting.]

34. There is further the difficulty of finding expression in adequate language for the intention of the legislator. Even the internal legislation of states suffers under this difficulty in so far as the art of legislation is still very clumsy and undeveloped. For international legislation there is in addition the further difficulty that different groups of peoples employ very different methods in

drafting their laws. If we were to give to an Englishman, a Frenchman, and a German the task of drafting a law upon the same topic, and if they were provided with the point of view from which the regulation of individual points was to proceed, so that the intention of the draftsmen would be the same, three very different drafts would nevertheless emerge. The English draft would deal in the most concrete manner possible with the situations to which it meant to apply; it would adduce as many particular cases as possible, and so would run the risk of forgetting some series of cases altogether. The German draft would be as abstract as is possible, and would entirely disregard individual cases, except such as required a special treatment; and so it would expose itself to the danger that in practice cases would be brought within the enactment which were outside the intention of the legislator. The French draft would attach more weight to principles than to individual points, enunciating principles in a legislative manner and leaving it to practice to construct out of these principles the rule for the particular case. Now, seeing that French is the language of international legislation, and so in the editing of drafts at the Hague Conferences the lion's share will naturally fall to French jurists attending the Conference, it will scarcely be possible to prevent the French method of legislation from obtaining great influence over international legislation. But there is no need for this mode of legislation to become dominant. The jurist representatives of other states must see to it that the French method is perfected by their own; the English and the Germans must make it their business to bring the drafts into a more concrete form, and to split up principles into more abstract rules. In this way, it may in time be possible by means of common international labour to make essential advance in the art of legislation.

[Sidenote: These difficulties distinct from those due to carelessness.]

35. But the difficulties inherent in the legislative method must not be confused with those which come from a careless employment of the method; the latter must always be avoided, otherwise we arrive at contradictions of interpretation, and these are insuperable.

[Sidenote: Article 23 (h) of the Hague Regulations of land war is an example.]

An example of such carelessness is afforded by the incorporation--at the second Hague Conference--of a new provision in the former Article 23 of the

'Regulations respecting the laws of land warfare'. I am referring to the provision added under the letter (h), which runs as follows: [It is forbidden] 'to declare extinguished, suspended, or unenforceable in a court of law, the rights and rights of action of the nationals of the adverse party'.

[Sidenote: The German and the English interpretation of Article 23 (h).]

36. From the German memorandum on the second Peace Conference it is quite clear that this additional rule, which was proposed by Germany and adopted by the Conference, was directed to the alteration of the rule, prevailing in several states, whereby during a war the subjects of one belligerent lose in the country of the other belligerent their persona standi in judicio, and the like. It is in this sense, then, that the addition has been unanimously interpreted by German literature, with the agreement of many foreign writers. The official standpoint of England, on the contrary, is that Article 23 (h) has nothing whatever to do with the municipal law of the belligerent countries. Article 23 (h), so the English Foreign Office explains, forms a subdivision of Article 23, which itself comes under the second section (headed 'Hostilities') of the Regulations, and forbids a series of acts which otherwise might be resorted to in the exercise of hostilities by the members of the contending armies, and by their commanding officers. That this interpretation is the right one--so it is further explained by the English side--is shown by the fact that Article 1 of the Convention expressly says, with reference to the 'Regulations respecting the laws of land warfare', that the contracting parties shall issue to their armed land forces instructions which shall be in conformity with the 'Regulations respecting the laws of land warfare' annexed to the Convention. It would therefore be the duty of every contracting power to instruct the commanders of its forces in an enemy's country (among other things) not 'to declare extinguished, suspended, or unenforceable in a court of law, the rights and rights of action of the nationals of the adverse party'.

[Sidenote: Davis's interpretation of Article 23 (h)]

37. This is also the opinion of Davis, one of the American delegates to the second Hague Conference; he gives the following explanation with regard to Article 23 (h), in the third edition of his Elements of International Law (New York, 1908), p. 578:

In this article a number of acts are described to which neither belligerent is permitted to resort in the conduct of his military operations. It was the well-understood purpose of the Convention of 1899 to impose certain reasonable and wholesome restrictions upon the authority of commanding generals and their subordinates in the theatre of belligerent activity. It is more than probable that this humane and commendable purpose would fail of accomplishment if a military commander conceived it to be within his authority to suspend or nullify their operation, or to regard their application as a matter falling within his administrative discretion. Especially is this true where a military officer refuses to receive well-grounded complaints, or declines to consider demands for redress, in respect to the acts or conduct of the troops under his command, from persons subject to the jurisdiction of the enemy, who find themselves, for the time being, in the territory which he holds in military occupation. To provide against such a contingency it was deemed wise to add an appropriate declaratory clause to the prohibitions of Article 23. The prohibition is included in section (h).

[Sidenote: Impossible to reconcile the divergent views about Article 23 (h).]

38. If, from the fact that Davis was an American delegate, we may conclude that he represents the government view of the United States of North America, we are confronted by the fact that official England and America adopt an interpretation of Article 23 (h) which is entirely at variance with that of Germany, and it is quite impossible to build a bridge of reconciliation between the two camps. This regrettable fact has its origin simply in the careless use of the legislative method. If the German conception of Article 23 (h) be the correct one, the lines of subsection (h) ought never to have found a shelter in Article 23, for they have not the slightest connexion with hostilities between the contending forces. If, on the other hand, the Anglo-American interpretation be the right one, pains should have been taken to secure a wholly different draft of the provision in question, for the present wording is by no means transparently clear. The protocols of the Conference (Actes, i, 101; iii, 14, 103) are not sufficiently explicit on the matter. The German delegate, G鰭pert, did indeed explain (cf. Actes, iii, 103) at the session of the first subcommission of the Second Commission on July 3, 1907, 'that this proposal is in the direction of not limiting to corporeal goods the inviolability of enemy property, and that it has in view the whole domain of obligations with the object of forbidding all

legislative measures which, in time of war, would deprive an enemy subject of the right to take proceedings for the performance of a contract in the courts of the adverse party'. But we shall scarcely go wrong if we assume that the members of the Second Commission, who were entrusted with the consideration of the 'Regulations respecting the laws of land warfare', had not sufficiently realized the full meaning of the German proposal. It would otherwise be quite unintelligible that the reporter upon the German proposal could say (cf. Actes, i, 101): 'This addition is deemed a very happy attempt to bring out in clear language one of the principles admitted in 1899', for these 'principles' (concerning the immunity of the private property of enemy subjects in land warfare) have very little indeed to do with the question of the persona standi in judicio of an enemy subject.

[Sidenote: Difficulties due to the fact that international law cannot be made by a majority vote, or repealed save by a unanimous vote.]

39. A difficulty of a special kind besets international legislation, owing to the fact that international rules cannot be created by a majority vote, and that, when once in existence, they cannot be repealed save by a unanimous resolution.

[Sidenote: A way out found in the difference between universal and general international law.]

But when once we free ourselves from the preconception that the equality of states makes it improper for legislative conferences to adopt any resolutions which are not unanimously supported, there is nothing to prevent a substantial result being arrived at even without unanimity. At this point the difference between general and universal international law furnishes a way out. Rules of universal international law must certainly rest on unanimity. It is postulated in the equality of states that no state can be bound by any law to which it has not given its consent. But there is naught to prevent a legislative conference from framing rules of general international law for those states which assent to it and leaving the dissentient states out of consideration. If the inclusion in a single convention of all the points under discussion be avoided, and if the method, adopted at the second Peace Conference, of dividing the topics of discussion among as many smaller conventions as possible be followed, it will always be found possible to secure the support of the greater number of states for the regulation of any given matter. In no long time thereafter the dissentient states will give in their adherence to these conventions, either in their existing or some amended form. Attention will then be paid also to the consolidation of several smaller laws in a single more comprehensive statute. The nature of the case and the conditions of international life call for concessions without which no progress would be practicable. The course of international legislation hitherto shows unmistakably that the trodden path is the right path. And it must be emphasized that it is open to a state to assent to an act of international legislation although some one or other provision thereof be unacceptable to it. In such a case the assent of the state in question is given with a reservation as regards the particular article of the Act, so that it is in no wise bound by that article. Numerous instances of this could be adduced: thus, at the Hague Conference of 1907 Germany withheld her assent to some of the proposed rules of land war, and England to certain articles in Conventions V and XIII.

[Sidenote: International laws which are limited in point of time.]

40. So also, the difficulty is not insuperable as regards the other point, namely, that international enactments when once in existence cannot be repealed or amended save by a unanimous resolution of the participant states. Here, too, the analogy between municipal and international legislation must not be pushed too far. Municipal legislation can at any time be annulled or altered by the sovereign law-maker; but international legislation, for want of a sovereign over sovereign states, is not open to such treatment. Here there is a way out, which was in fact adopted at the second Peace Conference, and also at the Naval Conference of London, namely, the enactment of laws so limited in duration to a period of years, that at the expiry of the period every participant state can withdraw. In this way, for example, it was agreed that the law about the International Prize Court and the Declaration of London should only be in force for twelve years, and that any of the powers which were parties thereto might withdraw twelve months before the expiry of that period, and that, if and as far as no withdrawal ensued, these laws should from time to time be continued in force automatically for a further period of six years. This kind of international legislation, with its time limit and the right of denunciation, is to be recommended wherever more or less hazardous legislative experiments are being made, or where interests are at stake which in course of time are liable to such an alteration as obliges states to insist on

the amendment or repeal of the previously made law. For example, the International Prize Court as a whole, and its composition, constitution, and procedure in particular, form an unparalleled experiment. But the fact that its institution is only to be agreed on for a period of twelve years facilitates its general acceptance, because of the possibility of either abrogating it altogether, or of reforming it, should experience show this to be necessary.

[Sidenote: International legislation no longer to be left to mere chance.]

41. However this may be, one point must be decisively emphasized,-- international legislation can no longer be left to mere chance. Apart from the Declaration of London and the Geneva Convention, it has always hitherto been a more or less happy chance which has controlled international legislation. Of conscious legislative consideration and deliberation, based on far-reaching, thoroughgoing preparation, there is no trace. For example, the Declaration of Paris of 1856 was but a by-product of the Peace of Paris of the same year. So also the legislation of the first Peace Conference was simply due to the anxiety to accomplish something positive which might conceal the fact that the proposed aim of the Conference--general disarmament, to wit--had in no wise been realized. At the second Peace Conference we did indeed see individual states appear with some well-prepared projects of legislation, but the preparation was entirely one-sided on the part of the states in question, and not general; accordingly, the adoption, rejection, amendment, and final shaping of these projects were also none the less the result of chance. The second Peace Conference itself took steps to prevent a repetition of this, calling the attention of the powers in its Final Act to the necessity of preparing the programme of the future third Conference a sufficient time in advance to ensure its deliberations being conducted with the necessary authority and expedition:

In order to attain this object the Conference considers that it would be very desirable that, some two years before the probable date of the meeting, a preparatory committee should be charged by the Governments with the task of collecting the various proposals to be submitted to the Conference, of ascertaining what subjects are ripe for embodiment in an international regulation, and of preparing a programme which the Governments should decide upon in sufficient time to enable it to be carefully examined by each country.

42. In contrast to the rules of the Peace Conferences, a really notable and exemplary preparation took place in connexion with the Declaration of London, and the befitting result was a law excellent alike in matter and in form. England, the state which summoned the Naval Conference of London, made a collection of the topics which would arise, and communicated it to the states attending the Conference with the request that they would send in full statements on the subjects mentioned. After the answers to this request had come in they were collated with regard to each of the points on which discussion would arise, and bases de discussion were elaborated which made a thorough examination of each point possible at the Conference. By this means it was at once made clear when the different states were in accord and when not. The door to compromise was opened. And apart from a few vexed questions an agreement was in this way successfully reached with regard to a comprehensive law resting at every point on exhaustive deliberation.

[Sidenote: The preparation of the Declaration a pattern for future international legislation.]

43. This model method must be the method of the future. If, as indicated in ?6 above, Art. 5, a permanent commission for the preparation of the Peace Conferences be successfully inaugurated, it will be its task to make preliminary preparations for the legislative activity of the Conferences in the manner just sketched out, and chance will no longer have the same part to play as heretofore. International legislation will no longer produce anything so full of gaps as the 'Regulations respecting the laws of land warfare', which leave essential matters--for instance, capitulations and armistices--without any adequate regulation.

[Sidenote: Intentionally incomplete and fragmentary laws.]

44. Of course, where the interests of different states are still involved in some uncertainty, or are in such antagonism that a complete agreement is impossible, even the fullest preparation and most painstaking deliberation will not procure a more satisfactory treatment for many matters than that the legislation which regulates them should be (so to say) only experimental and intentionally incomplete and fragmentary in character. Thus, for example, the Conventions

about the conversion of merchantmen into men-of-war and about the use of mines in naval war can only be considered as legislative experiments, regulating these matters merely temporarily and in an incomplete and unsatisfactory manner. But even conventions which designedly are full of lacunae have their value. They embody all the same an agreement upon some important parts of the respective topics, and provide a regulation which in every case is better than the chaos previously prevailing in the areas in question. They also constitute a firm nucleus round which either custom or future legislation can develop further regulation.

[Sidenote: Interpretation of international statutes.]

45. But even if international legislation attains the degree of success suggested, there still remains another great difficulty which must indirectly influence legislation itself, and that is the interpretation of international statutes once they have been enacted. It is notorious that no generally received rule of the law of nations exists for the interpretation of international treaties. Grotius and his successors applied thereto the rules of interpretation adopted in Roman law, but these rules, despite their aptness, are not recognized as international rules of construction. It can scarcely be said, however, that insurmountable difficulties have arisen hitherto out of this situation, for the majority of treaties have been between two parties, and the interpretation thereof is the affair of the contracting parties exclusively, and can be ultimately settled by arbitration. But in the case of general or universal international enactments we have to deal with conventions between a large number of states or between all states, and the question, accordingly, now becomes acute.

[Sidenote: International differences as regards interpretation.]

46. The difficulty of solving this question is increased by the fact that jurists of different nations are influenced by their national idiosyncrasies in the interpretation of enactments, and are dependent on the method of their school of law. Here are contrarieties which must always make themselves powerfully felt. The continental turn of mind is abstract, the turn of the English and American mind is concrete. Germans, French, and Italians have learnt to apply the abstract rules of codified law to concrete cases; in their abstract mode of thought they believe in general principles of law, and they work outwards

from these. English and Americans, on the contrary, learn their law from decided cases--'law is that which the courts recognize as a coactive rule' is an accepted and widely current definition of law in the Anglo-American jurisprudence; they regard abstract legal rules, which for the most part they do not understand, with marked distrust; they work outwards from previously decided cases and, when a new case arises, they always look for the respects in which it is to be taken as covered by previous cases; they turn away as far as possible from general principles of law, and always fasten on the characteristic features of the particular case. If continental jurists may be said to adapt their cases to the law, English and American jurists may be said to adapt the law to their cases. It is obvious that this difference of intellectual attitude and of juristic training must exercise a far-reaching influence on the interpretation and construction of international enactments.

[Sidenote: Different nations have different canons of interpretation.]

47. It is because of what has just been explained that the rules for the interpretation of domestic legislation are different with different nations. For example, whilst in Germany and France the judge avails himself more or less liberally of the Materialien[1] of a statute in order to arrive at its meaning, the English judge limits himself to the strict wording of the text, and utterly refuses to listen to an argument based on the historical origin of the statute. The English bench, sticking more closely to the letter of the law, allows also an extensive or restrictive interpretation thereof much more seldom than the continental judiciary does.

[1] It seems impossible to find any single English phrase which gives the meaning of Materialien in this context. In the Materialien of a statute is comprised everything officially put on record concerning it between the time the draftsman undertakes to draft the measure and the time it is placed on the statute-book. For instance, the commentary which a draftsman on the Continent always adds to his draft, giving the reasons for the provisions of the Bill; the discussions in Parliament about the Bill; and the like.-- TRANSLATOR.

[Sidenote: Controverted interpretation of the Declaration of London an example.]

48. A good illustration of the factors under consideration was furnished by the movement in England against the ratification of the Declaration of London, and the discussion evoked thereby in the press and in Parliament. It was asserted that many rules of the Declaration were so indefinitely framed as to lie open, castle and keep, to the arbitrary inroads of a belligerent interpreter. And when the advocates of ratification pointed to the official 'General Report presented to the Naval Conference by its Drafting Committee', which gave a satisfying solution to the issues raised, the answer came that neither a belligerent nor the International Prize Court would be bound by the interpretation of the Declaration contained in this General Report. It was asserted that the ratification of the Declaration would refer only to the text itself, and that the General Report, not being thereby ratified, would not be binding; only by express extension of the ratification to the General Report could the latter bind.

Continental jurisprudence, if my conception of it be correct, would stand shaking its head at the whole of this discussion. It would ask how there could be any talk of ratifying a report, ratification having only to do with agreements. And as regards the question of the binding character of the General Report, there might indeed be some objection on the Continent to the epithet 'binding', but, on the other hand, there would be no doubt that the interpretation of the Declaration given in the Report must be accepted on all sides. The Report expressly says:

We now reach the explanation of the Declaration itself, on which we shall try, by summarizing the reports already approved by the Conference, to give an exact and uncontroversial commentary; this, when it has become an official commentary by receiving the approval of the Conference, would be fit to serve as a guide to the different authorities--administrative, military, and judicial-- who may be called on to apply it.

Seeing that the Conference unanimously accepted the Report, there is expressed in it and by it the real and true meaning of the individual articles of the Declaration as the Conference itself understood and intended it. Every attempt to procure an inconsistent interpretation must come to grief on this fact, and so the Report is in this sense 'binding'. The ratification of a treaty extends, of course, not only to the words themselves, but also to their meaning, and if the Conference which produces an agreement itself unanimously applies a definite meaning to the words of the agreement, there cannot remain any doubt that this is the meaning of the verbal text. Nevertheless, the contrary was maintained in England by a party of men of legal eminence, and the explanation of this is only to be found in the fact that these English lawyers were applying to the interpretation of the Declaration the rules which govern the interpretation of English statutes. The only way to enable the English Government to ratify the Declaration seems to be a statement by the Powers at the time of ratification that the interpretation of the Declaration expressed in the General Report is accepted on all sides.

[Sidenote: Some proposals for the avoidance of difficulties in interpretation.]

49. However this may be, the illustration adduced is sufficient proof that the interpretation of international enactments creates a difficulty of its own for international legislation. International legislators must bring even greater solicitude than municipal legislators to the expression of their real meaning in rigid terms. And this aim can only be attained by the most assiduous preparation and consideration of the contents of the enactment. It would be best if these contents were published and thereby submitted to expert discussion before they were finally accepted at the Conferences. The national jurisconsults of the participant states would thus be enabled to criticize the proposals and to indicate the points which especially need clearing up. It might also be possible to consider the enactment, by convention, of an international ordinance containing a series of rules for the interpretation and construction of all international statutes. This much is sure, that the interpretation of international statutes must be freer than that of municipal statutes, and must therefore be directed rather to the spirit of the law than to the meaning of the words used. This is all the more requisite because French legal language is foreign to most of the states concerned, and because it is not to be expected that before ratification they should obtain minute information about the meaning of every single foreign word employed.

CHAPTER III

INTERNATIONAL ADMINISTRATION OF JUSTICE

[Sidenote: Law can exist without official administration.]

50. It is inherent in the nature of law that it should be put in question whenever from time to time one party raises a claim in the name of the law which the other resists in the name of the same law. If, however, it be asserted that there cannot be any law where there is no official administration of justice, this is a fallacy, and the fallacy lies in considering the presence of the elements of the more perfect situation to be presupposed in the less perfect situation. Beyond a doubt it is the administration of law which gives law the certainty that its authority will in every case obtain operative effect. But this operative effect is obtainable even apart from administration, because those who are subject to the law are in most cases clear as to its contents, and so they raise no question about it, but submit to its application without any need of recourse to jurisdictional officials. All the same, when a dispute does arise, law needs official administration: and, accordingly, in the long run, no highly developed legal society can dispense with it.

[Sidenote: The Hague Court of Arbitration as a permanent institution.]

51. Until the end of the nineteenth century the society of states possessed no organ which made international administration of justice possible. When states had made up their mind to have a dispute between them settled amicably, they either appointed the head of a foreign state or a foreign international jurist as arbiter, or they selected a number of persons to form an arbitral tribunal. It was a great step forward when the first Hague Conference established a Permanent Court of Arbitration and agreed on international rules of procedure for the conduct of this court. And if, seeing that in every particular instance the court is ultimately chosen by the parties, the expression 'Permanent Court of Arbitration' is only a euphemism, nevertheless the permanent list of persons from among whom the arbiters can be chosen, and, in addition, the Permanent Bureau of the Court of Arbitration at The Hague, and, lastly, the international rules of procedure, represent at least the elements of a permanent court. Thereby an institution is obtained which is always available if only parties will make use of it, whereas such an institution was entirely lacking formerly, and if parties wanted an arbitration they had to enter on lengthy arrangements about the machinery of the process. And the short experience of twelve years has already shown how valuable the institution is, and how well adapted to induce disputant states to make use of it.

[Sidenote: The proposed International Prize Court and Court of Arbitral

Justice.]

52. The second Peace Conference took, however, another great step forward in the resolution to establish an international court of appeal in prize matters, and also in the proposal about a really permanent international court to exist by the side of the Court of Arbitration. And the United States of North America have recently entered on negotiations with the object of utilizing the International Prize Court, should it come into existence, as at the same time a permanent tribunal for all legal issues. Here present and future touch hands, and these proposed institutions must therefore be discussed. Attacks upon them have been made from two sides, it being asserted that they infringe the principles of the equality and sovereignty of states.

[Sidenote: Does the constitution of the International Prize Court violate the principle of the equality of states?]

53. It is alleged that the principle of equality is violated in that the Prize Court is contemplated as consisting of fifteen members, so that, while the eight Great Powers are always represented by a member, the thirty-seven smaller states are only represented by seven members who take their seats in the court in rotation according to a definite plan. Now it is not clear how the principle of equality can be deemed violated thereby. This principle has really nothing to do with the constitution of an international court so long as no state is compelled to submit itself to such a tribunal against its will. It would be possible to constitute an international court without basing it on the representation of definite states, and that is very likely to come to pass in the future, when fuller confidence in the international judicature is felt. In the proposed composition of the Prize Court expression is given, undoubtedly, to the actually existing political inequality of states, a matter which, however, has not the least connexion with their legal equality. This political inequality will never disappear from the world, and if in course of time the creation of an international judicature is really intended, the realization of this idea is only possible subject to the existence of political inequality. There is little doubt that when we come to the constituting of the Prize Court certain smaller states will abstain because no permanent representation therein is allotted to them. But it may confidently be expected that the recalcitrant states will give in their adherence in the future, when they begin to see what beneficent results the institution has produced.

[Sidenote: Does the International Prize Court restrict the sovereignty of the several states?]

54. The International Prize Court violates the sovereignty of states just as little as it violates the principle of equality. No state submitting itself to an international tribunal submits itself thereby to the power of any other earthly sovereign so long as no other power is entrusted with the execution of the awards of the international tribunal, that is to say, so long as submission to any such award rests always and entirely on the voluntary submission of the state concerned. If this be not correct, then there would also be an invasion of sovereignty whenever--as indeed happens everywhere more or less--a state submits itself to the decrees of its own courts, and allows its subjects an appeal to its courts against the measures of the government. In the latter, as in the former case, what we have is merely the demission to the determination of the court of the question whether certain acts and claims are consistent with law. He who at the present day conceives sovereignty as an unlimited arbitrariness of conduct is guilty of an anachronism which is everywhere contradicted by the mere fact that there are such things as international law and constitutional law.

[Sidenote: Would the formation of an international Prize Court of Appeal infringe the sovereignty of the several states?]

55. It is next alleged that there is a violation of sovereignty in the fact that the proposed Prize Court is a court of appeal which is to be competent to reverse the decisions of national prize courts. There is nothing in this objection also, for it rests on a petitio principii. If we but get rid of the preconception that a sovereign state can only admit an interpretation of law to be authoritative for itself when pronounced by its own courts, no reason is visible why an award of an international court which upsets an award of a national court should be considered an infringement of state sovereignty. He who alleges it to be an infringement has really in view, however unconsciously, the power of execution which is inherent in the decrees of a national court, and he is unable to conceive a judicial decree without power of execution. Judicial declarations of law have, however, as little as the essence of law itself to do with power of execution; otherwise--as indeed happens in the case of many persons--the law of nations must be denied any legal character. Now, just as that system of law

is more complete behind which there stands a central authority enforcing it by compulsion, so also that judicial activity is more complete with which physical power of execution is conjoined. But alike in the one and in the other case, physical power is not an essential element in the conception. Just as there is law which in point of fact is not enforceable by any central authority, so there can also be jurisdictional functions without any correlative power of execution. International administration of justice is, in the nature of the case, dissociated from any power of this kind; therefore, too, it does not impair the sovereignty of states.

[Sidenote: The powers of the International Prize Court do not curtail state-sovereignty.]

56. It is imagined that a trump card is played when it is asserted that Article 7 of the Convention, entered into at the second Peace Conference, respecting the Prize Court, curtails state-sovereignty when it provides that, in default of definite agreement and of generally recognized rules of the law of nations, the Prize Court is to give its decisions in accordance with the principles of justice and equity, and that therefore (so the assertion continues) on certain points the Prize Court can make international law by itself. Whilst up to the present time custom and convention have been the two sources of the law of nations, the Prize Court--so it is said--is now to be added as a third, and the law made by it is to become international law without requiring the assent of the several states. All this argument rests on a false assumption. The article in question endues the Prize Court in certain points with a law-making power which is simply a delegated power. The states which are concerned with the Prize Court desire, in the interests of legal security, that the tribunal should not declare itself incompetent by reason of want of existing rules on any given matter. They accordingly delegate to this tribunal the power which lies in them collectively of making rules of international law, and they prospectively declare themselves at one with regard to the rules which the tribunal shall declare to be binding in the name of justice and equity. Now the Prize Court is not hereby made a special and independent source of international law by the side of convention, but the law which it declares is law resting on an agreement between states. Even in the inner life of states we meet with delegation of legislative power to a limited degree, and yet this does not mean that the authorities in question are raised into special and independent sources of law side by side with the government of the state. And just as in the inner life of a

state a delegation of legislative power does not involve an infringement of sovereignty, so also the delegation of legislative power to the Prize Court involves no infringement of the sovereignty of the members of the international community of states.

[Sidenote: Difference between international courts of arbitration and real international courts of justice.]

57. The step from the International Court of Arbitration to the erection of a real international court is, on two grounds, a decided step onward. In the first place, an arbitral tribunal is not a court in the real sense of the word, for its decisions are not necessarily based on rules of law, and it does not necessarily deal with legal matters. An arbiter, unless the terms of the reference otherwise provide, decides ex aequo et bono, whilst a judge founds his decision on rules of law and is only applied to on legal issues. Valuable as it may be in many cases to withdraw a matter from the courts and remit it to arbitration, it is in other cases equally valuable to have a cause decided in legal fashion by a judge. The experience which we have so far had of arbitral tribunals shows that they make praiseworthy efforts to arrive at a finding which shall as far as possible satisfy both parties, and that they have in view a compromise rather than a genuine declaration of law. Now the cases are, all the same, numerous enough in which the parties want a real, genuine declaration of law, and so it would be most valuable if a real international court were in existence. In the determination to erect an International Prize Court it has been recognized that prize cases ought not to be brought, from occasion to occasion, before an arbitral tribunal and there peaceably arranged, but ought to be decided by a real court on the basis of the law of prize. If success attends the attempt to convert the Prize Court into a general international court or if a special international court is created, this would render it possible to have other international legal disputes also decided by a real court upon naked principles of law. Such a possibility is in the interest of the parties and also in that of international law itself, for it will be held in higher and surer esteem if a court is provided for its authoritative interpretation and application.

[Sidenote: Fundamentals of arbitration in contradistinction to administration of justice by a court.]

58. The second ground referred to is that it is a fundamental part of the idea

of arbitration that in every case the choice of the arbiters as men in whom the parties have confidence should be left to the parties themselves, whilst it is fundamental in the conception of a court that it is once and for all composed of judges appointed independently of the choice of the parties and permanently to adjudicate upon matters of law. Such a court secures continuity of jurisprudence, affords a guarantee for the most exact examination of questions of fact and of law, deems itself to a greater or a less degree bound by its previous decisions, contributes thereby to the settlement of open legal questions, and furthers the growth of law while adding to the respect in which it is held. Nothing can heighten the respect in which international law is held more than the existence of a real international court.

[Sidenote: Opposition to a real international court.]

59. But, incredible as it may sound, this is not generally recognized. It is just among the old champions of the arbitral decision of international disputes that the most violent opposition is raised to the erection of a real court of justice for international law causes. In such a court they see a great danger for the future. The fact that arbitration has a tendency to furnish rather a decision which is as far as possible satisfactory to both parties than one which is based on naked law, is just the respect which, in the eyes of many, gives it a higher value than a real court possesses. Not jural but peaceable settlement of disputes is the motto of these men; they do not desiderate justice in the sense of existing law, but equity such as contents both parties. And they gain support and approval from those who see in the law of nations rather a diplomatic than a legal branch of knowledge, and who therefore resist the upbuilding of the law of nations on the foundation of firmer, more precise, and more sharply defined rules on the analogy of the municipal law of states. These persons range themselves against an international court because such a court would apply the rules of the law of nations to disputed cases in the same way in which the courts of a state apply the rules of municipal law to disputed cases arising within the state; they prefer diplomatic or, at any rate, arbitral settlement of disputes between states to the purely legal decision thereof. They also contend that an international court without an international power of execution is an absurdity.

[Sidenote: A real international court does not endanger the peaceable settlement of disputes.]

60. This last objection has already been dealt with above (paragraph 55), where it is shown that a judicial award as an authoritative declaration of the legitimate character of an act or claim has, in and for itself, nothing to do with the governmental execution of the award. But as to the fear that the erection of an international court might endanger the peaceable settlement of disputes and the development of international arbitration, that is certainly groundless. The contrary is the case, as is shown by the fact that the happy movement towards the erection of an international court was initiated by the United States of North America. This country, which since its entry into the international community of states has more than any other championed the idea of the arbitral adjustment of disputes, and has in practice put it to good use, is well aware of the value of arbitration, but, on the other hand, it knows also how to prize the purely legal decision of legal questions. It has actually happened that a state has not ventured to submit a certain dispute to arbitration because it feared that its claim would not receive jural treatment in this way. It is just because the existence of an international court would promote the non-warlike settlement of international claims that its erection has been put forward. The reason is that even with the most careful selection of arbiters, one is never certain beforehand as to the quarter whence they will derive their ideas of the aequum et bonum, whilst with a jural settlement of claims the decision rests on the sure basis of law. Further, the erection of an international court is not intended to cause the suppression of the so-called Permanent Court of Arbitration; on the contrary, the machinery of this latter is to be retained in full existence, so that the parties may in every case be able to choose between the Court of Arbitration and a real court. The future will show that both can render good service side by side.

[Sidenote: Composition of an international court.]

61. If the erection of an international court comes to pass, the equipment of it with competent and worthy men will be of the highest importance. Their selection will have difficulties of all sorts to overcome. The peculiar character of international law, the conflict between the positive school and the school which would derive international law from natural law, the diversity of peoples (consequent on diversity of speech and of outlook on law and life) and of legal systems and of constitutional conceptions, and the like--all these bring the danger that the court in question should become the arena of national

jealousies, of empty talk, and of political collisions of interest, instead of being the citadel of international justice. All depends on the spirit in which the different governments make the choice of judges. Let regard be paid to a good acquaintance with international law joined to independence, judicial aptitude, and steadfastness of character. Let what is expected of candidates be the representation not of political interests but of the interests of international jurisprudence. Let nomination be made not of such diplomatists as are conversant with the law of nations, but of jurists who, while conversant with this branch of law, have had the training required of members of the highest state judiciary, and have been tested in practice. Let men be chosen who are masters not only of their own language and of French, but also of some other of the most widely diffused languages, and who possess an acquaintance with foreign legal systems. If this be done, all danger will be avoided. Judges so selected will speedily adapt themselves to the milieu of the international court and be laid hold of by it, and their equipment for their task completed. As things are at present, the institution of an international court is an unheard-of experiment. But the experiment must be made at some time, and the hope may be confidently entertained that it will be successful. Petty considerations based on the weakness of humanity and doubts as to the sincerity of the efforts of states to submit themselves voluntarily to international tribunals must be silenced. Fear of international entanglements and groupings is misplaced. National prejudices and rivalries must keep in the background. The big state's disdain of the little state and the little state's mistrust of the big state must give place to mutual respect. Opposed to the hope and confidence that the experiment will succeed there are no considerations other than those which have been arrayed against every step forward in international life. They will disappear like clouds when the sun of success has once begun to shine upon the activity of the International Court.

[Sidenote: International courts of appeal a necessity.]

62. Obviously it will not be possible in the long run to stop at a single international court; the erection over the court of first instance of an international court of appeal is also a necessity. The proposed Prize Court will indeed be itself a court of appeal because it cannot be approached until one or two national courts have spoken. But the proposed International Court of Justice would be a court of first instance. Now there are no infallible first-instance decisions. Even courts are fallible and make mistakes. If this is

universally recognized for municipal administration of justice, it must be recognized for international administration of justice, all the more as public and not private interests are then in issue. If states are to feel bound to rely on their right rather than on their might, and to submit it to a judicial decision, it must be possible to carry an appeal against a decision of the International Court of Justice to a higher tribunal. Many advocates of arbitration will not hear of an appeal. In this they may be right as regards a real arbitral decision given ex aequo et bono, but their arguments lose all force before the nakedly jural decision of a real court.

The difficulties which beset the erection of an international court and the appointment of its members may lead to the renunciation of the immediate establishment of an international court of appeal. But when once the International Court is in active working, the demand for a court of appeal will be raised and it will not be silenced until it has been satisfied. It would be premature to make proposals now as to the manner in which such a court of appeal ought to be composed, and as to the way in which it could be brought into existence. It is enough to have pointed to the need for it. Directly this need makes itself felt, ways and means will be found for supplying it.

[Sidenote: Are international courts valueless if states are not bound to submit their disputes to them?]

63. We next are faced by the objection, what possible value can the establishment of international courts possess if it be optional to states either to submit their causes to them or to rely on arms for a decision of those causes? It is, accordingly, asserted that such courts can only be of value if states place themselves under a permanent obligation to submit to them all or at any rate the greater number of their disputes. This leads to the question of obligatory arbitration treaties, which played so prominent a part at the second Peace Conference, and will surely come up again at the third Conference. I have not the slightest doubt that the third or some later Conference will agree on the obligatory reference of certain disputes between states to arbitration, but the matter is of quite subordinate importance so far as the erection of international courts is in question. Any one who contemplates international life and the relations of states to one another, without prejudice and with open eyes, will see quite clearly that, when once there exist international courts, states will voluntarily submit a whole series of cases to them. These will, at first,

admittedly, be cases of smaller importance for the most part, but in time more important cases will also come to them, provided that the jurisprudence developed in them is of high quality, and such as to give states a guarantee for decisions at once impartial and purely jural and free from all political prepossessions. It is the existence of the institution which is the vital question now. Once the machinery is there, it will be utilized. In all states of the world there are movements and forces at work to secure the ordered and law-protected settlement of international disputes. The existence of an international court will strengthen these movements and forces and render them so powerful that states will scarcely be able to withdraw themselves from their influence. And the time when states were ready to draw the sword on every opportunity belongs to the past. Even for the strongest state war is now an evil, to which recourse is had only as ultima ratio, when no other way out presents itself.

[Sidenote: What is to be done if a state refuses to accept the decision of an international court?]

64. In conclusion the great question is, what is to happen if a state declines to accept the decision of the international court to which it has appealed?

Important as this question may be in theory, it is a minor one in practice. It will scarcely happen in point of fact--assuming that there is an international court of appeal above the court of first instance--that a state will refuse a voluntary acceptance of the award of an international court. Only slowly, and only when irresistibly compelled by their interests so to do, will states submit their disputes to international courts. But when this is the case these same interests will also compel them to accept the award then made.

[Sidenote: Executive power not necessary for an international court.]

65. We have neither desire nor need to equip these courts with executive power. In the internal life of states it is necessary for courts to possess executive power because the conditions of human nature demand it. Just as there will always be individual offenders, so there will always be individuals who will only yield to compulsion. But states are a different kind of person from individual men; their present-day constitution on the generally prevalent type has made them, so to say, more moral than in the times of absolutism. The personal interests and ambition of sovereigns, and their passion for an

increase of their might, have finished playing their part in the life of peoples. The real and true interests of states and the welfare of the inhabitants of the state have taken the place thereof. Machiavellian principles are no longer prevalent everywhere. The mutual intercourse of states is carried on in reliance on the sacredness of treaties. Peaceable adjustment of state disputes is in the interests of the states themselves, for war is nowadays an immense moral and economic evil even for the victor state. It may be that a state will decline to submit its cause to the international tribunal because it thinks that its vital interests do not allow such submission; but when, after weighing its interests, it has once declared itself ready to appear before the court, it will also accept the court's award. All other motives apart, the strong state will do this, because its strength allows it to make voluntary submission to the award, and the weak state will also do so because war would be hopeless for it.

[Sidenote: Right of intervention by third states and war as ultima ratio.]

66. If, however, in spite of all, it should happen that a state declined such acceptance of an award, the powers who were not parties would have and would use the right of intervention. For there can be no doubt of the fact that all states which took part in the erection of an international court would have a right to intervene if a state which entered an appearance before an international court should refuse to accept its award. And of course, in such a case, war is always waiting in the background as an ultima ratio; but it is in the background only that it waits; while, apart from the erection of an international court, it is standing in the foreground. The whole problem shows that the development in question cannot be rushed, but must proceed slowly and continuously. Step can follow step. The economic and other interests of states are more powerful than the will of the power-wielders of the day. These interests have begotten the law of nations, have driven states to arbitration, have called forth the establishment of a Permanent Court of Arbitration at The Hague, and are now at work compelling the erection of international courts. Let us arm ourselves with patience and allow these interests to widen their sway; they will bring about a voluntary submission to the judgments of the international court on the part of all states.

CHAPTER IV

THE SCIENCE OF INTERNATIONAL LAW

67. International organization and legislation and the establishment of international courts are the business of the Hague Peace Conferences; but to work out the new enactments and to turn them to good account and to prepare for their practical application, this is the business of the science of international law. Science obtains thereby a share in the future of the law of nations, and quite new tasks are allotted to it. As mentioned earlier, the law of nations was, until the first of the Peace Conferences, essentially a book-law. Treatises depicted the law such as it was growing, in the form of custom, out of the practice of states in international intercourse. There were only a few international enactments, and there was no international court practice. But that state of things has now been altered once and for all. International enactments appear in greater number. Decisions of international courts will follow, just as we already possess a number of awards of the Permanent Court of Arbitration. If science is to be equal to its tasks, it must take good heed to itself, it must become wholly positive and impartial, it must free itself from the domination of phrases, and it must become international.

68. It is indispensably requisite that this science should be positive in character. What natural law and natural law methods have done for the law of nations in the past stands high above all doubt, but they have lost their value and importance for present and future times. Now and onwards the task is, in the first place, to ascertain and to give precision to the rules which have grown up in custom, and in the second place to formulate the enacted rules in their full content and in their full bearing. In doing so it will come to light that there are many gaps not yet regulated by law. Many of these gaps may be successfully filled up by a discreet employment of analogy, but many others will remain which can only be remedied by international legislation or by the development of customary law in the practice of the courts or otherwise. What science can do here is to make proposals de lege ferenda of a politico-jural character, but it cannot and may not fill up the gaps. Science may also test and criticize, from the politico-jural standpoint, the existing rules of customary or enacted law, but, on the other hand, it may not contest their operation and applicability, even if convinced of their worthlessness. It must not be said that

these are obvious matters and therefore do not need special emphasis. There are many recognized rules of customary law the operativeness of which is challenged by this or that writer because they offend his sense of what is right and proper. As an example thereof let us take the refusal by some well-reputed writers to include annexation after effective conquest (debellatio) among the modes, known to international law, of acquisition of state territory. They teach that debellatio has no consequences in point of law, but only in point of fact; that it rests on naked might and brings the annexed area under the power of the victor only in point of fact and not in point of law. Here they are putting their politico-jural convictions in the place of a generally recognized rule of law.

[Sidenote: The science of international law must be impartial.]

69. Science cannot, however, be genuinely positive unless it is impartial and free from political animosities and national bias. To believe that it really is at present impartial is a great deception. Whoever compares the writings of the publicists of the several states runs up against the contrary at every step. There is no state which in the past has not allowed itself to be guilty of offences against international law, but its writers on international law seldom admit that this has been the case. They perceive the mote in the eye of other nations, but not the beam in the eye of their own nation. Their writings teem with ungrounded complaints against other nations, but scarcely throw the slightest blame on their own country. By such a method problems are not brought nearer to solution, but only shoved on to one side. What is wanted, is that an ear should be lent to the principle audiatur et altera pars, that the opponent should be heard and his motives weighed. It will then often turn out that what was believed to merit reprobation, as a breach of law, will show itself to be a one-sided but forceful solution of a disputed question. And even where a real breach of law has been committed it will be worth while to weigh the political motives and interests which have driven the perpetrator to it. It must ever be kept in mind that at the present day no state lightheartedly commits a breach of the law of nations, and that, when it does commit such a breach, it is generally because it deems its highest political interests to be in jeopardy. Such a weighing of motives and interests does not mean excusing the breach of law, but only trying to understand it.

[Sidenote: The science of international law must free itself from the tyranny of phrases.]

70. It is also indispensable that the science should free itself from the tyranny of phrases. As things are, there is scarcely a doctrine of the law of nations which is wholly free from the tyranny of phrases. The so-called fundamental rights are their arena, and the doctrines of state-sovereignty and of the equality of states are in large measure dominated by them. Any one who is in touch with the application of international law in diplomatic practice hears from statesmen every day the complaint that books put forth fanciful doctrines instead of the actual rules of law. Now it is often not difficult to push the irrelevant to one side and to extract what is legally essential from the waste of phrase-ridden discourse. But there are entire areas in which the tyranny of phrases so turns the head that rules which absolutely never were rules of law are represented as such. Two conspicuous examples may serve to illustrate this statement.

[Sidenote: The meaning of 'Kriegsron geht vor Kriegsmanier'.]

71. My first example is taken from the use made of the German maxim 'Kriegsr 鈼 on geht vor Kriegsmanier'. This maxim is a very old one, and there was nothing in the law of nations which stood in the way of its unreserved acceptance so long as there was no real law of war, but the conduct of war rested only on a fluctuating number of general usages. The meaning of 'manier' is 'usage', and 'Kriegsr 鈼 on geht vor Kriegsmanier' means that the usages of war can be pushed aside when the reason of war demands it. At the present day, however, the conduct of war is no longer entirely under the control of usages, but under the control of enacted rules of law to be found in the 'Regulations respecting the laws of land war', and the application of the old saw to these legal rules can only lead to abuses and erroneous interpretations. What it says is, in short, nothing else than this: If the reason of war demands it, everything is permissible. But since the first Hague Peace Conference that is definitely no longer the case. Article 22 of the 'Regulations respecting the laws of land war' expressly says that belligerents have not an unlimited right of choice of means of injuring the enemy. Kriegsr 鈼 on, therefore, cannot justify everything. Some enacted rules about the conduct of war are, indeed, framed with such latitude as to allow scope for the operation of Kriegsr 鈼 on. But most of them do not leave it any scope, and they may not remain unobserved even if Kriegsron were to make it desirable. It must be admitted that the general principle of the law of nations, that such acts as are absolutely

necessary for self-preservation may be excused even though illegal, is applicable to the law of war also. And, further, in the exercise of justified reprisals, many enacted rules of war can be set aside. But mere Kriegsron never extends so far as to dispense with enacted rules of war. Nevertheless numerous well-reputed German authors teach the contrary, and even those who perceive the falsity of this doctrine still retain the old saying and identify Kriegsron with the narrower idea of military necessity. If we are to arrive at clearness, if possible abuses are not to receive in advance the sheltering protection of law, the maxim 'Kriegsron geht vor Kriegsmanier' must disappear from the science of international law. It has lost its meaning and has become an empty but dangerous phrase.

[Sidenote: The doctrine of Rousseau concerning war.]

72. My second example is taken from the use to which an assertion of Rousseau is commonly put. In his Contrat Social, Bk. I, ch. iv, is the following passage: 'War, then, is not a relation of man to man, but a relation of states in which private persons are enemies only accidentally; not as men nor even as citizens, but as soldiers; not as members of their country, but as its defenders. In a word, each state can only have as enemies other states and not men; seeing that no true relation can exist between things of different natures.'

It is in this assertion of Rousseau that a basis is found for a quite common doctrine to the effect that war is a relation only between the belligerent states and their contending forces. See how much else has been deduced from this principle and demanded on the strength of it! That blockade is only permissible in the case of naval ports and fortified coast-towns, and not in the case of other ports and places. That breach of blockade is as little punishable as carriage of contraband, seeing that it is but a commercial act of peaceable individuals, it being immaterial whether they are subjects of a neutral power or of the enemy. That the capture of enemy merchant vessels on the high seas is unlawful, because these vessels are dedicated to peaceful trade alone, and have naught to do with hostilities. That peaceful intercourse, and especially commercial intercourse, between the subjects of the belligerents cannot be forbidden. And more of the same kind.

If now we examine more closely, we find that there is a sound principle at the core of Rousseau's doctrine, but that the sentence 'war is merely a relation between the belligerent states and their contending forces' is an empty, untenable phrase. The sound central principle is that in fact, according to modern conceptions, war is a struggle between the belligerent states, carried on by means of their military and naval forces, and that their subjects can only be attacked or taken prisoners so far as they take part in hostilities, and that, if they behave quietly and peaceably, they are spared harsh treatment as far as possible. But to assume on that account that a war in which his state is engaged does not affect a subject, and that he is not brought thereby into hostile relations to the other side so long as he abstains from any active part in hostilities--this deals a blow in the face to all the actual facts of war. Certainly, a peaceable subject does enjoy exemption from avoidable severities, but he is none the less the object of coercive measures. If at the outbreak of a war he be resident in the territory of the enemy, cannot he be expelled? If he contribute to a loan raised by the enemy, will not his own state punish him for treason? Is it not the law of many states that if they go to war, an end is put to peaceful intercourse, and especially commercial intercourse, between their own subjects and the subjects of the enemy state? Must not the private person submit to requisitions, pay contributions, endure limitations on his freedom of movement, and obey the commands of the hostile occupant? Is not his property on many occasions--for example, during a siege or a bombardment, or on the field of battle--destroyed without compensation? Must he not, if his fatherland is completely conquered and annexed by the enemy, reconcile himself to becoming a subject of the enemy? Whoever has lived in a district occupied by an enemy knows what an empty phrase the assertion is, that war is not a hostile relation between a belligerent state and the subjects of its enemy. Yet the phrase, nevertheless, wanders from book to book and from mouth to mouth, and must always be available whenever wanted in order to justify some assertion which contradicts the recognized rules of warfare. The kernel of truth in Rousseau's doctrine is this, that while the soldier is put in an actively hostile position, the peaceable subject of a belligerent is put in a passively hostile position; but the doctrine is absolutely misunderstood, although the distinction which it asserts is quite commonly recognized. And so here also it must be repeated that, if we are to arrive at clearness, if baseless claims are not to appear under the cover of law, the phrase 'War is only a relation between the belligerent states and their contending forces' must disappear, as being misleading, from the science of international law.

[Sidenote: The science of international law must become international.]

73. It is, finally, a pressing necessity that the science of international law should become international. The science of international law is essentially a branch of the science of law, and it can only thrive if this dependence be not suppressed. Now the science of law must, of necessity, be a national one, even if at the same time it employs the comparative method. On this ground the science of international law, forming always a part of a national science of law, must in this sense be national. When, despite this, I insist that it must become international, what I have before my eyes is merely the requirement that it should not limit itself to the employment of national literature and the jurisprudence of national courts, and that it must make itself acquainted with foreign juristic methods.

[Sidenote: Necessary to consult foreign literature on international law.]

74. There is as yet scarcely any systematic reference to foreign literature on international law. Monographs may possibly cite the old editions of some wellnigh obsolete text-books, but, with individual laudable exceptions, there is scarcely any suggestion of the real utilization of foreign literature. This defect is, admittedly, to be attributed not so much to writers themselves as to the fact that foreign literature is for the most part inaccessible to them. There ought to be in every state at least one library which devotes especial attention to international law, and makes, on a well-elaborated plan, a judicious collection of foreign literature on the subject, particularly foreign periodicals.

[Sidenote: Necessary to understand foreign juristic methods.]

75. In worse plight than even the employment of foreign literature is the understanding of foreign juristic methods. And yet without such an understanding the gates are thrown open for misconceptions, for unfounded claims, and for mutual recriminations. How great is the divergence of juristic method can only be appreciated by one who has practised and been called to the teaching of law in different countries. Now, just as the outlook of its people is incorporated in the law of every state, so the specific mode of thought and the logical attitude of any given people are mirrored in its juristic methods. Historical tradition, political interdependence, and other accidental influences do indeed also play a great part therein, but the fundamental factor is the difference of modes of thought and points of view. Seeing, then, that the

law of nations is one and the same for every member of the community of states, but that on the other hand the science of every state elaborates the law of nations on the basis of its national juristic methods, it is unavoidable that discord should arise if the science of international law of individual states neglect to acquaint itself with foreign juristic methods. It is not only in scientific treatises, but also in judicial decisions, that expression is given to these methods, and the discordance between judicial decisions on the same issue given in different states is often traceable simply to the difference of juristic method. That the law is essentially the same is no guarantee that in all countries there will be a unanimity of judicial pronouncement on every point thereof. If ever--and it is not outside the range of practical possibility--an international agreement, including all states, were arrived at concerning all the topics of the so-called international private law and international criminal law, there would, for the reason under consideration, still continue to be no security that the same law would in every point receive the same treatment from the courts of all countries. In order to attain this end there would have to be an international tribunal erected above the municipal courts of all states, and its judgments would have to be accepted as binding by the municipal courts concerned. It is just for this reason that the proposed International Prize Court and the proposed permanent court for international disputes will aim in the course of their practice at securing an identical application of the rules of the law of nations. And the joint labours of judges of diverse nationalities in these international courts will influence their mutual understanding in a manner which will be serviceable to the juristic methods of the different peoples.

CONCLUSION

[Sidenote: The aims defended are not Utopian.]

76. We have reached the end. I have conducted the reader over wide areas, and have put before him aims which cannot be immediately attained. But these aims are not on that account nebulous and Utopian. We are already on the way which leads to them, even though a long time will still be required before we draw quite near. This hope may be with certainty indulged in, because the forces at work for the organic development of the community of states are ever gathering strength. The governments of states may continue an obstinate opposition to these forces, but in the end they must give way. Economic interests primarily, but many others also, prevent individual states from

allowing the international community of states to remain unorganized any longer. Slowly indeed, and only by degrees, and to a large extent unwillingly and of compulsion, but nevertheless step by step, states will be impelled onwards towards a goal still in part unknown. It is amusing to observe the parts which individual states play in this process of development. At one time it is one power, and at another time another power, that is led by its interests to seize on the leading role, and make progressive proposals. At one time a progressive proposal is joyfully welcomed, at another it is declined, at another time it meets with partial assent and partial dissent. In the matter before us the United States of North America play a very prominent part; they have the merit of having taken a most conspicuous share in the development of the law of nations, especially of the law of neutrality. It was America that moved for the erection of a permanent international court, and in any event she will not give up the idea even if she cannot secure its speedy realization.

[Sidenote: Obstacles to progress.]

77. Favourable as the auspices are for continuous progress, there are not wanting, on the other hand, influences and circumstances opposed to progress.

In the first place, there is national chauvinism, to which the existence of a law of nations is hateful, and which represents unlimited national self-seeking. Where It obtains the upper hand, International conflicts are unavoidable, and cannot be composed by a judicial sentence. In the second place, there is the fact that the political equilibrium, on which the whole law of nations rests, presents itself as a system liable to gradual as well as to sudden alteration. Were the earth's surface permanently divided between equally great and equally powerful states, the political equilibrium would be stable, but it is rooted in the nature of things that this equilibrium can only be unstable. The reason is that individual states are subject to a perpetual process of evolution, and thereby to perpetual change. This evolution is for one state upwards, for another downwards. No state is permanently assured against break-up, and it is the break-up of existing states and the rise of new states that threaten the permanent organization of the international community of states with danger. There is also another factor demanding attention, and that is the opposition between West and East, although the glorious example of Japan shows that the nations of the East are indeed capable of putting themselves on the plane of Western civilization, and of taking a place in the sun in the international community of states.

However this may be, we must move onward, putting our trust in the power of goodness, which in the course of history leads mankind under its propitious guidance to ever higher degrees of perfection.

###

www.ingramcontent.com/pod-product-compliance
Lightning Source LLC
Chambersburg PA
CBHW070920180526
45168CB00005B/2092